frogments
from the frag pool

haiku after bashō

selected titles by gary barwin

Doctor Weep and other strange teeth (The Mercury Press, 2004)
a periodic table of the alphabet (serif of nottingham, 2004)
Raising Eyebrows (Coach House Books, 2001)
Seeing Stars (Stoddart Kids, 2001)
Big Red Baby (The Mercury Press, 1998)
Outside the Hat (Coach House Books, 1998)
Cruelty to Fabulous Animals (Moonstone Press, 1995)
The Mud Game (with Stuart Ross; The Mercury Press, 1995)

selected titles by derek beaulieu

fractal economies (Talonbooks, 2006)
the orange manifesto (MODL Press, 2005)
fractals (No Press, 2005)
Calcite Gours (Writers Forum, 2005)
With Wax (Cuneiform Press, 2004)
[Dear Fred] (above/ground, 2004)
with wax (Coach House Books, 2003)
Velvet Touch Lettering (yardpress, 2003)

frogments
from the frag pool

haiku after bashō

gary barwin & **derek beaulieu**

THE MERCURY PRESS

The publisher gratefully acknowledges the financial assistance of the Canada Council for the Arts, the Ontario Arts Council, the Ontario Media Development Corporation, and the Ontario Book Publishing Tax Credit Program. The publisher further acknowledges the financial support of the Government of Canada through the Department of Canadian Heritage's Book Publishing Industry Development Program (BPIDP) for our publishing activities.

Editor: Angela Rawlings
Composition and page design: Angela Rawlings
Cover design: Angela Rawlings
Cover image: Gary Barwin

Printed and bound in Canada
Printed on acid-free paper

1 2 3 4 5   09 08 07 06 05

Library and Archives Canada Cataloguing in Publication

Barwin, Gary
    Frogments from the frag pool : haiku after Basho / Gary Barwin, Derek Beaulieu.
ISBN 1-55128-112-0

    1. Haiku, Canadian (English). 2. Canadian poetry (English)--21st century. I. Beaulieu, D. A. (Derek Alexander), 1973- II. Title.
PS8553.A783F76 2005   C811'.0410806   C2005-905292-9

The Mercury Press
Box 672, Station P, Toronto, Ontario Canada M5S 2Y4
www.themercurypress.ca

This water-sound is intended for the haiku-master or entity to which it is addressed, and may contain confidential and/or privileged material. If you are not the intended recipient of this water-sound, you are hereby notified that any use, review, retransmission, dissemination, distribution, reproduction, or any action taken on reliance upon this water-sound is prohibited. If you received this water-sound in error, please contact the leaper and delete the material from any poem. Any views expressed in this water-sound are those of the individual frog and may not necessarily reflect the views of the pond.

(every(all at(toge(frog)ther) once)thing)

furu ike ya
kawazu tobikomu
mizu no oto

— Matsuo Bashō (1644-1694)

The old pond;
A frog jumps in —
The sound of water.

— Translated by R.H. Blyth

email to basho

re:pond
respond

old pond leaping
into mind of frog

old pond leaping —
the mind of frog

old frog
leap from the water
soundlessly
still the rippling mind

old pond
sound fond
frog find

the body is 98% water
each cell a tiny pool

basho, i said
you sit in silence

yes, he said
a billion frogs
make little sound

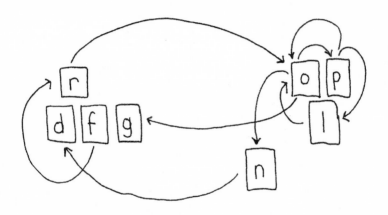

leaping water —
the mind ponding
frog sound

old pond
sound in mind of frog —
pond-old and unsound —
teach again the mind to leap

frog, you are old as i
the old leaps flagging
the weary mind

frond-friend
the watersongs sound fallow
without you

old(((((((((((frog)))   )   )   )   )   )pond

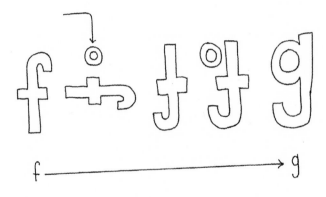

old pond
it's a good thing it wasn't
a rhinoceros

1. splash
2. 17th-century japan
3. a riverside house in edo
4. matsuo basho 1644-1694
5. a frog-shaped opening
6. a frog
7. an old pond
8. paper
9. a reed pen
10. no mind
11. an instant

basho
frog in the throat
leaps in the mind

frogs on fronds in the bogpond
loghop leap lilypads pools

throngs plodding sodden sink sudden o'er bog brink
think bogfrog fog songs sound cool

moon over pond

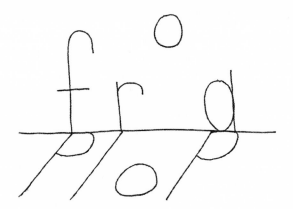

(evening)

pond holding
its breath

the frog

old pond
universes rise & fall
a single splash

basho
i asked

but what if we weren't
ready?

as og is to ond, he said
you'd get the water's lash

water-shaped hole in silence
frog-shaped hole in pond

poem shaped hole in mind

old pond
cracking

the frog in winter


```
   old (     )
       (     ) pond
       (     )
 water (     )
       (     )
       (     ) sound

       (frog)
```

integeribbit

p^{3}o^{3}ndfrgl

after basho

```
    o
   p│nd
  f r│g
  pl│ p
    ↓
    o
```

numbered series

1.

fr   old   og
spl   po   ash   nd

spl   old   ash
po   fr   nd   og

spl
    fr
      ash
        og

spl   old   ash   po   fr   nd   og

2.

fr   sp   og   lash
spl   fr   ash   og

spl   fr   as   og   h
o   spl   ld   as   po   h   nd   pl   fr   op   og

3.

b   spl   ash   o

spl   b   ash   o   g   ld   p   fr   on   d   g

old man
asleep by the pond
toad told the tale

2 haiku

fr fl ay og   to sp ad f lash
spl fl fr ay ash

o pl ld op : po fr nd og
old fr spl po ash og nd

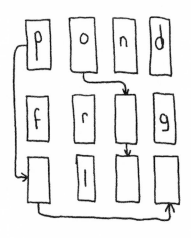

frog longing
the pond-old sound
of water lapping

basho

trembling

as

water

ripples

frogs

leap

over

his

grave

in the mind of pond
frog is an opening

in the mind of frog
the pond opens

the splashed mind

one fun young tongue sung song saying
pond-sound song frond-friend frog finds fine for frog fall fable

in the mind of frog
haiku

basho's pond

to	and	fro
to(ad)	and	fro(g)

basho's enlightenment

p	OH!	nd
fr	OH!	g
pl	OH!	p

old pond
frog-leap-in
the tiny splash
soaking stars

ol   po
wa   so
a   fr

o   o
w   s
a   f

.ld   .nd

.er   .nd

.og

pondensation

opwsaf

f pp

roo l

o lno

gddp

basho inflamed

extinguished by
water-sound

                                  b
                                    o
              s   p   f r   g
                    l
                 a   a
                 y   s
                          h

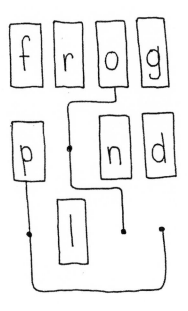

old frog
fold
pond

old plash
frond

old ash
splond

frold ash
splog

fold splash
pond

                                        tadpold
                                        tadpond
                                        tadplop
                                        tadpole

old pond draws the line
frog crosses it

frogment of bashogination
pondment of frognition
ploperty of water

frog
despondent

pond
respondent

pond
frog resplendent

other pond
other frog
same plop

circinate fronds of a young fern
circumscissle pod of plantain
chthonic chuckle-head

once ponded a tide
the moon out
a frog sponding to it
a-ponded, apon'd it

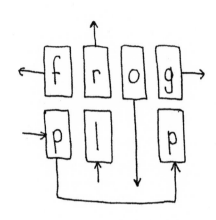

basholation

O

─────────

O

oldpond
frogplo
poldpo
ndfro
gplo
pol
dp
o
n
d

a

———————

a

splsh

———————

o

frg

———————

ol   po

wa   (   )   so

a   fr

before nightfall
frog fall

old pond
the moon's pool

so much noise
a single fall

gravity ponding a frog
frogging a pond
holding basho to the ground

basho
you shift vowels
sound the certain splash

a frog leaps into a pool of light

o   o
  ae — ou
a   o

from nowhere
a frog dives down onto
a watery planet

now the rippling stars

old frog
leap-splash this:

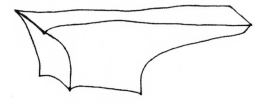

the frog leaps
leaves a lilypad
to remember

old pond
frog weeping:
water sound

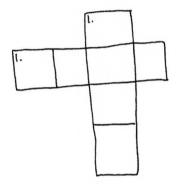

<u>down.</u>
1. warted basho.

<u>across</u>
1. smooth basho.

a leap in the dark
lit by an old man's way

a leap in the dark
an old man's way

a leap in the dark
lights an old man's way

basho
frogs on the brain

also
the universe

ripples in water
memories of tadpole youth

basho
frog shift

the sounds remain
the fronds refrain

ripples (in glass houses)

a. throwing stones

b. jumping frogs

zen basho

```
  p0nd
+ fr0g
  pl0p
─────────
     0
```

somes

```
1 x f
1 x r
3 x o
1 x g
3 x p
1 x n
1 x d
1 x l
─────────
```

bash0

corrupted haiku

chinese
water
torture

noah's shaken as
the frog leaps in

**basho's bonanza: a love
poem for lorne green**

pond
eros
a

**basho's place in the
catholic church**

supreme pondiff

splash of
green-eyed monster

i've pushed
basho into the pond

surprised by a frog
of course! a jewish man, i've
no foresight either

aquarium

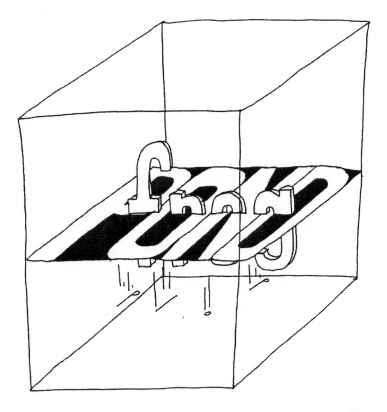

frond
pop
plog

frop
pog
plond

frnd
oplpo
plnd

ripples

p (o) n d
f r (o) g
p l (o) p

( )o( )( )
( )( )o( )
( )( )o( )

((o)))
(((o))
(((o))

basho's nipples

```
( )( )   ( )( )
( ((o))((o)) )
( )( )   ( )( )
```

plague

```
p       f   f
o         r  pr
np   p o  oo  f
doppleganger
 nolo    d   o
  dnop        g
  dp
```

plagued by word 6.0

oxy-acetylene welding nutshell;
noxious dope-fiend —
non-transparent dixieland.

**microsoft word thesaurus
reads basho**

pool;
frog in one's throat —
drops noisily.

old pond
has frogs
also
time

old pond
stars
frogs

old computer
crash!
no frogs

pond
frog

frondship

basho was proclaimed a god in the buddhist pantheon

by the way

pond puzzle filled with
frog-shaped piece


```
                pond
             po(frog)nd
              po(    )nd
             po(        )nd
            po((        ))nd
           po(((        )))nd
          po((((        ))))nd
         po((((        ))))nd
```

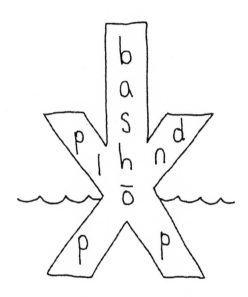

no pond
frog jumps
on paper

frog lounging:
the pond
just before the plop

old pond
frogmenting
"the greatest basho on earth"

pond
ponder

pondest

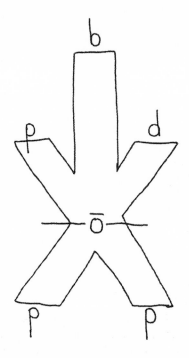

glyph

an alphabetic transposition and gloss

source:

> old pond
> water sound
> a frog

where a=b:

> pme qpoe
> xbufs tpvoe
> b gsph

line 1:
pme, the sound of poem — pome — the o a tiny pond, a moon risen from the lips and then lost by cloud, or pme, pomme as if o its picture felled by arrow off the head of a frightened child.

qpoe, kapow — the sound of arrow hitting apple, qpoe, poetry truncated, 'try' broken off, q the p reflected in a pool of water, as if p poetry tried suddenly tried to turn its head.

line 2:
xbufs, x marks the spot where the confident father aimed, the spot where the young saint ended his alphabet, the teacher marking x: wrong. bufs — buffs, aficionados, they've taken a shine to it, then later, ex-buffs, their enthusiasm dimmed, gone cloudy, they've polished it off and now regret it, x crossing it out, taken the apple back.

tpvoe, typed over it, typo vers (fr.), voe — no sibilance in their 'voice,' voe calling out as the arrow hits the mark, kapow. no time for reflection now. too late to cut it short, diving first, then thinking of water.

line 3:
b, an existential imperative, the apple bisected, the command follows. b, speckled with droplets of water, apple juice, the moon covered by clouds in the mist. gsph the gasp as the apple falls, as the cold water closes, as the poem is thought of, the sudden breath like gsph, a gospel remembered, the young saint writing, coming to x like a glyph.

vowels

shift

beneath

you

yet

you

beneath

shift

vowels

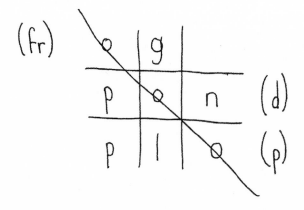

old frog
wart found
a polyp!

toad
lasered
a frog reborn!

old pond on TV
rippling

do not adjust
your set

the pond will not be televised

old pond TV:
a TV
in the pond
on the TV
an old pond
in the pond
another TV
someone holds up a sign
frogs fall like mice from heaven

frog leaps
into wet jacket
disturbs the fronds of style

frog leaps
under bridge

of old man's nose

from *haiku night in canada*

moon a yellow puck
poet plops frog into pond
yes: he shoots. he scores.

o
frog leaping
into the centre of
itself

old pond
no gravity
frog leaps over the surface
of sound

gravity
splashes
(in)
an old man's mind

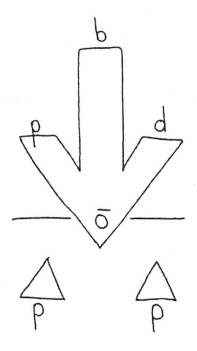

basho / human / frog / water

"i have had this splash
since
i was young"

pond asks basho
to imagine
a frog

basho hears frog
imagines pond

pond hears basho
imagines frog

not pond-sound
ear-sound

it's not the splash
but that
the frog leaps

old pond
wants to be
left alone

old pond
remembers only
one frog

frog sleeps:
the sound of pond

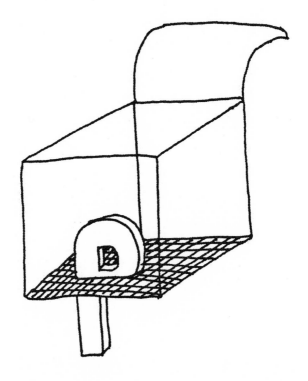

a frog jumps

the division of pond and frog breaks down

the pond is identical in size and shape to the frog

in its formative stages the pond was a drop of water. seeing it suddenly glisten, one could easily have mistaken it for a tadpole

the pond leaps, surrounding the frog like a raincoat

it is believed that the pond opened before the actual and apparently sudden impact of the frog as the frog ponds, the pond frogs

the moment of illumination is not that instant when the frog hits the surface of the pond

it is that moment when the frog knows it is going to leap, that moment when the pond prepares to open. it is that moment when the path between frog and pond first finds its form, arching from lily pad to the filigreed edge of broken meniscus

we are deceived by the sound of water

yo-yo by pondside

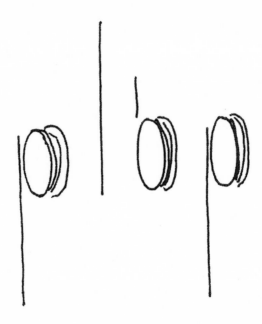

pond dreams
by the sound
of frog

frog leaps
ha!
mouth opens

water sound
someone's pulled
the frog
from under me

frog:
pond bound

ponderous

pl O p

p O nd

fr o g

old pond
a patient eye
a frog

skinner's poem
typing a line
reach the end and
a bell goes off

skinner's pond
bell rings
frog drops

frog
skinner dipping

furu ike ya
kawaku tobikomu
mizu no oto

furtive glance
kangaroo court
mitigation

fierceness frozen water dog sound
keel toasted koala
misuse may choose

old saws

you can't teach
an old pond
new frogs

you can lead a mind to a pond
but you can't make it leap

a frog in the mind
is worth
two in the pond

a leap in the pond
is better than
two minds

the frog never
leaps
far from the splashed mind

the water never
lands far from
the frog

you can't teach
eveningness
to an old pond

Re-evaluating *Silence on the Frogpond*

In 1985, W. Hood published *Silence on the Frogpond*, a
work that proved to be extremely influential in the field of
molecular poetics. He states that:

> old pond
> no sound
> a frog

He asserts that frog and pond do not come into contact.
Indeed, he states, the molecules of the pond and frog are
positioned in such a way that they do not collide but rather
pass by each other.

— frog/pond model proposed by W. Hood, 1985

However, Hood's model fails to consider the observed release
of energy during the frog/pond interaction. If, as Hood's
model contends, the molecules of the frog and pond are to

interpenetrate, then some further explanation is required in order to explain the discrepancy in total energy. When the molecules intersect, the bonds of attraction, due to Van der Waals forces, are broken. How are we to account for this "missing" energy? Where does it go?

After extensive research into this problem, a solution of startling simplicity has been discovered. The "missing" energy can be accounted for by taking into consideration neurological change in the observer — the same neurological change observed by M. Basho all those years ago in his seminal work of 1674:

> leaping water —
> the mind ponding
> frog sound
> — M. Basho (1644-1694)

Precise measurements are unavailable as there are currently an insufficient number of reproducible results. Further, a dependable means of accurately determining how much energy is released into the cortex during this interaction has not been devised. In preliminary research, measurements of up to 5.3 units Basho (international Basho standard: 1 Basho = 575 kilojoules) have been recorded, but this figure needs to be substantiated by independent researchers.

Additionally, further research remains to be undertaken from the perspective of motivational analysis. Johnston (1986) has theorized that the energy present in the mind of the frog can be considered as resulting in the leap, but, as we have suggested elsewhere (Barwin and beaulieu, 1987), we must more closely examine the role of the pond in creating the leap. Investigation of this kind will certainly be met with much skepticism, for it goes against the current belief that, in the words of one anonymous poet:

> old pond:
> mere plop

Continued research of this important area needs to be completed if we are to dispel this superficial view. We are confident that further study will provide us with more specific data concerning the dynamics of the frog/pond interaction and prove conclusively that frog, pond, and human are linked by their intrinsic interdependence.

BASHOGRAPHY

Barwin, Gary and beaulieu, derek. "Pond Regards to the
Frog." *The Journal of the International Bashological
Society.* Vol. 27, No. 4 (1987). 46-54.

Hood, Wharton. *Silence on the Frogpond.* Toronto:
Plopologics Press. Monograph No. 24 (1985).

Johnston, Herman. "Analysis of Cortical Change in Leaping
Frogs." *Frog Kinetics Journal.* Vol. 7, No. 18 (1986).
34-45.

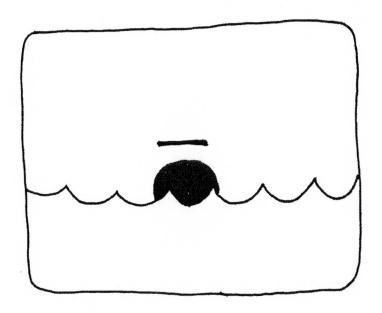

old man
leaps
follows an idea
into the pond

old pond
malaplop!
the green toed

old pond
frog jumps in

homelessnessless

old pond
frog

listlessnessless

do-it-yourself aha moment

old pond

                    something;
                    something somethings —
                    something.

old pond
plop
some frog

dlo dnop
polp
a gorf

Frog at the Bar

The sky was threatening to burst and so I ended up at Sam Meniscus' Bar before the usual time. Met this old guy nursing a drink at a table at the back. He was looking to talk, and time had almost run out on his beer.

"It's about seeing," he said. "And about not seeing." His watery eyes were rheumy ponds, and his whole body trembled slightly as he spoke. "You see the rain out there? Imagine trying to see a single drop fall, trying not to see any of the other drops. That's what I had to do. That's what I had to accomplish. And it wasn't easy. You think it was easy?"

I drained my bourbon. Motioned to the barman for another. "Don't figure so."

"Well, that's how it was with the frogs. Thousands of the things. All burping, and bubbling, and hopping all over the place. It wasn't easy to ignore them, the warty buggers. Slimy green jumping rats. So I sees this one frog and I train my eye on him. Trick was to ignore all the other frogs. The first couple of hundred times I lose him quick. But I go back to the pond for months. You think I had anywhere better to go? Think I'd hang around the station waiting for the goddamn bus to the friggin' Deep North? Not this gutterball. So the weather's getting cold. We're all moving slow — me, the frogs, the girls plopping down grey stuff at the soup kitchen. So finally I blank out all the other frogs and stick my eye to the big mother frog. And then it jumps from its place on the slobbery bank. AND IT HITS THE GODDAMN SURFACE OF THE POND WITH A SOUND LIKE MY TEETH BEING PULLED OUT. The pop of the pink denture goo snapping off my I-don't-know-what-colour-they-are gums. I knew it would be like that. Perfect. A single island of pure uninterrupted sound in my sorry and always interrupted life. When I heard it I knew I'd been waiting for that sound ever since I was denture-cream pink and wrapped in diapers. And you know what I did? You'll never guess, not in a million. I ripped open some smokes and wrote on the package. In Japanese. A guy back at the bunk told me what it was. Five, seven, five. A haiku. Whatever the hell that means. I'd wanted to watch the frog, hear it crack open the pond. But what was the point? It's been almost four hundred years. I'm still trying to figure it out."

the frog is gone
its splash only reaches me now

frogknowledgements

"I will smite all thy borders with frogs."
— *Exodus* 8: 2-3

"andor think about translating some of the
other haiku that basho has written instead of
his stupid frog pond thing for crissakes"
— Darren Wershler-Henry, *the tapeworm foundry*

These poems res(pond) not only to Matsuo Basho's haiku, but
are equally homages to the translative work of Dom Sylvester
Houédard, Steve McCaffery, jwcurry, and bpNichol. Thanks
must be made for their teaching, poetry, and influence.

pieces and drafts of *frogments* have appeared:

derek beaulieu – through the following presses: housepress, kitsch in ink press, poemEpress, poetic immolation press; and in the following magazines: *The Capilano Review, Empty Galaxy, in grave ink, Laughing Gland, Peter O'Toole, RAW NerVZ HAIKU, Queen Street Quarterly, Polartis*; and online in *[sic]*.

Gary Barwin – in/on the following books, chapbooks, T-shirts: *Raising Eyebrows* (Coach House Books), *Outside the Hat* (Coach House Books), *Cruelty to Fabulous Animals* (Moonstone Press), *frogments from the fragpool* (Proper Tales Press), *Basho translation from Fragments from the Frogpond* (housepress), *Two Basho translations* (Flying Camel Editions), *Ukiah poems 4* (Underwhich Editions); and from the following (a)periodicals: *Geist, Rampike, Border/lines, Industrial Sabotage, sh'wipe, Toronto South Asian Review, Inkstone*.

Thanks to all those involved in the creation, distribution, and support of the above publications.

Gary Barwin is a writer, composer, and performer. His music and writing have been published and presented in Canada, the US, and Europe. He received a PhD in Music Composition and was the recipient of the 1998 KM Hunter Foundation Artist Award. *Seeing Stars*, a YA novel, was a finalist for both CLA YA Book of the Year, and an Arthur Ellis Award. He teaches creative writing courses at McMaster University and music

and creative writing at Hillfield Strathallan College. In addition to many vertebrate publications, he is the author of numerous invertebrates, many from his own serif of nottingham editions. Barwin lives in Hamilton, Ontario and online at garybarwin.com.

derek beaulieu has been an editor at both *filling Station* and *dANDelion* and special editor of *Whitewall of Sound* and *Open Letter*. In addition to his magazine editing work, he was the editor/publisher of housepress and is the author of several books of poetry, including *with wax* (Coach House Books, 2003). derek is also the co-editor of *Shift & Switch: New Canadian Poetry* (The

Mercury Press, 2005). His poetry, criticism, and artwork have appeared in magazines and galleries across Canada. He lives in Calgary with his young daughter.

Narrow Road from the True North

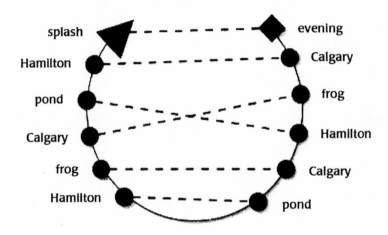